"*Sad Sally is a marvelous children's book with illustrations that lift the story of* and engaging way. Absolutely first rate! I cannot wait to read this book to m the best children's books I've seen in a long, long time."
    — Norm Foster, Canada's Top and Most Produced Playwright

"*A child having repressed pent up feelings of sadness and a censored edict to not open up, leads to severe depression and an inability to experience love and life's intimacy. Colleen Aynn's 'Sad Sally' is a beautiful highly relatable tool for any psychologist, or child/youth worker to alleviate such suffering in children that they're entrusted to treat. A must arrow in your therapeutic quiver!*"
    — Dr. Stephen B. Stokl, FRCPC, Chief Psychiatrist, Southlake Regional Health Centre, Author of *Mentally Speaking*

"*With a simple and heart-warming story,* Sad Sally *reminds all of us, young and old, of the importance of accepting our emotions and staying true to ourselves and to our feelings. Wonderful story with a great moral.*"
    — Liana Palmerio-McIvor, Registered Psychotherapist

"*Adults are reminded that sometimes kids just need you to listen, not explain away. And kids will know that sometimes you just need to go ahead and have the experience. Great work Colleen.*"
    — Dr. Norm Buckley, FRCPC, Director, Michael G. DeGroote National Pain Centre, Famous *Jeopardy* answer

"Sad Sally *is an adorable book and truly unique. This story will inspire children to recognize their real feelings and invite them to express them in a way that will bring about joy and positive change. I truly love this book!*"
    — Peggy McColl, New York Times Best-Selling Author, aka "The Best Seller Maker"
    peggy@peggymccoll.com, http://peggymccoll.com

"*Colleen has taken some very complex teachings about dealing with emotions, our subconscious mind, our dark side etc. and turned them into something very accessible and fun for both parents and children. Bravo! What a great tool to help us teach our children and ourselves more about our own feelings.*"
    — Judy O'Beirn, International Bestselling Author of *Unwavering Strength* series

"*I got really emotional when I read* Sad Sally. *It's a book that I wish I had read when I was a kid or that my Mom could've read with me. When I was little I had these overwhelming feelings, I didn't know what they were and I didn't know what to do with them. This would've been such a comfort. I highly recommend this book for every parent and child.*"
    — Dr. Bruno Borges, Pediatric Anesthesiologist, McMaster Children's Hospital

SAD SALLY

by

Colleen Aynn

Introduction

Sad Sally first showed up one night while I was onstage. I'm not an author by trade, I'm a performer, and I had gone back to work when my daughter was seven months old. She was super colicky, driving me crazy at home, and I just needed to get out of the house!

So, I was playing June Carter Cash in a Johnny Cash musical and one night under dramatically dim lighting, instead of writing 'Ring of Fire' for Johnny, I drew these little characters. I loved them. Every night after that, I would turn to a new page in my notebook and draw. By the end of the scene, this adorable group of little faces were looking up at me. I called them 'feelings friends'; Sad Sally, Mad Marlene (who later turned into Mad Michael), Happy Hannah, and Nervous Nelly.

I originally thought they were for my daughter, to help her process her feelings but looking back, I realize they showed up to help me process mine.

We're not really comfortable with 'negative' emotions. We're not taught how to deal with them. Growing up, the message I got about feelings was: just be happy, push aside the ugly feelings, and eventually they'll go away. Something in me knew this couldn't be overly healthy but I never had a very good alternative. I figured there were 'good' feelings and 'bad' feelings, and if I spent most of my time hanging out with the good ones, I'd be fine.

I ended up in therapy due to the colic and the first thing I learned is that repressing emotion – any emotion – is the worst thing you can do! It is actually the beginning of disease in the body. Feelings teach us a lot about ourselves and the world around us, if we take the time to listen. Feelings themselves are neither good nor bad. They just are. It's what we do with them that give them their positive or negative value.

'Good' emotions feel good so we mostly try to hang out there. The trouble comes when we realize we've never developed any skills for dealing with the 'negative' ones.

'Negative' emotions can be difficult because of how big they are, how uncomfortable they feel, how badly we've seen them expressed by others, and how many times we've fumbled our way through them ourselves. What I didn't know is the way you deal with sadness or anger can actually turn them into incredibly positive forces in your life.

It is my intention to give you a few more tools in your toolbox so you can express your negative emotions in a healthy manner and help the little ones in your life to do the same. It's my hope that in using these tools you will feel your happiness level and the happiness level of your entire family go up. I know I did.

Come on over to **www.colleenaynn.com** and say "hi"! I've got a cool spot called **#makesmefeel** where you and your kids can send me your pictures, drawings, art, photographs, books, Lego creations or anything that makes you feel your feelings! I'd love to see your creations and put them up so others can be inspired to express themselves too.

I believe in the healing power of creativity and expression. Here's to feeling our big feelings and putting them all to good use.

Your voice matters.

Much love,

C xo

For my daughter Emilia, the reason it all began.

She was sad when she walked to school all alone.

She was sad when she talked to her friends on the phone.

She was sad when her running shoes both came untied.
She was sad when it was time to go back inside.

She was sad when she went for a ride in the car.
She was sad when it finished and hadn't gone far.

Sally sniffled down the dusty old road.
She looked on the path and there sat an old toad.

"Look at you, eating flies, all covered with lumps.
Doesn't that just get you down in the dumps?"

"Why no!" said the frog. "It's just who I am."

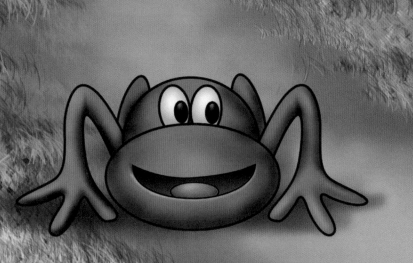

"Doesn't that make you sad? I don't understand.
I'm sad about everything!" she said with a tear.
"Not really sure why - I just can't seem to cheer."

"So cry! Let it out! Let the tears come and go.
Sob your sweet little heart out. Here's a tissue to blow."

Sally looked at him stunned. "Right now? You don't mind?"
"Mind? Not at all! I'll stand here by your side."

She sobbed long and hard. She cried deep and low.
She opened herself up and let those tears flow.
They flowed down her cheeks. They flowed from her eyes.
They flowed all around her from deep, deep inside.

And just when she thought she had no more to shed,
she scrunched up her face and she started again.

She cried out a river that turned into a lake.

She cried out more tears than she thought she could take.

One after one they fell from her eyes.
Then they stopped. She was shocked!

She had none left inside!

"What's happening here? I could cry tears galore!
Now my tears are all gone. Never felt this before.
I'm not feeling sad – I feel breezy and light.
I don't know what this is – am I doing it right?"

"You're doing just fine, even better I'd say.
Sounds to me like you're free!
What a wonderful day!"

The frog took her hand and looked deep in her eyes.

"When you see a rainbow way up in the skies, remember your rainbow and set yourself free. Take a deep breath. Feel however you please."

Sally felt her eyes well up with a tear,
but she didn't feel sad now.

She wanted to cheer!

"I'm feeling so different," she said with a smile.
"I'm feeling happy! Wow! It's been a while."

"I knew you could do it!" said the little green frog,
who hopped off to the meadow and back to his log.

About the Author

Colleen is a true artist. She has been (loudly) expressing herself since birth as an international singer, actor, author and coach. Believing that we are all born creative, Colleen inspires others to boldly express themselves and bring their unique voice to the world. You can find her on stages, in classrooms, behind canvases, or pianos with a pen, microphone or book in her hand.

Colleen has spent most of her life performing as a Musical Theatre Professional. After her daughter was born, she found herself on stage each night drawing tiny little characters that helped her understand and process her feelings. She designed the Feeling Friends series to help little minds deal with big feelings in a positive way for parents and children. Colleen still loves to get up on stage and belt out a tune and these days she's most often joined by her husband Bruno and little firecracker Emilia. Colleen lives in Burlington, Ontario Canada.

Printed by Amazon Italia Logistica S.r.l.
Torrazza Piemonte (TO), Italy

10508800R00020